THE JOURNEY CONTINUES VOL 8

WILLIAM HATFIELD

ACKNOWLEDGEMENTS

We are all on a journey through life! I want to thank all my family and friends who stand besides me and encourage me when times are tough.

I especially want to thank my aunt Viola for all her work in editing and preparing the manuscript of my first book for publishing. The knowledge she shared will help me to continue writing. Her confidence in me ignited a gift I never realized I had. God created me with many gifts and one of them is to be a writer. Thank you Jesus for your great love.

DEDICATION

I dedicate this book to the thirsty and hungry saints of God that desire an intimacy with the Holy Spirit like no other. My prayer is that you can find this journey as a source of encouragement, strength and power to overcome life's struggles and walk in a greater sense of freedom and relationship with the Holy Spirit and all within your sphere of influence.

PROLOGUE

Everybody is interested in the future and what does it hold for me. Questions are asked and internalized, meditated on and depending on the outcome of the meditation, reaction results. Our reactions are either fear based or faith based depending on the subject meditated on. I have always been interested in the ways of God rather than the acts of God. The ways of men don't escape the scrutiny of God. People can hide behind words and fool people. These statements came across my Facebook page and inspired me to research and write this book.

People be like: "She doesn't act like a Christian".
God be like: "I'm not looking for actors. I'm looking at the Heart".

CONTENTS

1 THE HEART

I am not discussing the heart as in the organ in our body that pumps blood through our system giving us life. I want to look at the central or innermost part of someone. There are many scriptures that mention heart but not as the physical organ. There are many Bible verses discussing the heart because God's word is clear that the condition of your heart is critical in your walk with the Lord.

Mark 11: 23 For verily I say unto you, That whosoever shall say unto this mountain, Be thou removed, and be thou cast into the sea; and shall not doubt in his **heart**, but shall believe that those things which he saith shall come to pass; he shall have whatsoever he saith. This is the heart I want to look at.

Matthew 6:**21** For where your treasure is, there your heart will be also.

Proverbs 3:**5** Trust in the LORD with all your heart and lean not on your own understanding;

Proverbs 4:23 Above all else, guard your heart, for everything you do flows from it.

Romans 12:2 Do not conform to the pattern of this world, but be transformed by the renewing of your mind. Then you will be able to test and approve what God's will is—his good, pleasing and perfect will.

Proverbs 23:26 My son, give me your heart and let your eyes delight in my ways,

Psalm 51:10 Create in me a pure heart, O God, and renew a steadfast spirit within me.

Psalm 73:26 My flesh and my heart may fail, but God is the strength of my heart and my portion forever.

Philippians 4:7And the peace of God, which transcends all understanding, will guard your hearts and your minds in Christ Jesus.

John 14:27 Peace I leave with you; my peace I give you. I do not give to you as the world gives. Do not let your hearts be troubled and do not be afraid.

Psalm 37:4 Take delight in the LORD, and he will give you the desires of your heart.

Job 9:4 His wisdom is profound, his power is vast. Who has resisted him and come out unscathed?

Psalm 9:1 I will give thanks to you, LORD, with all my heart; I will tell of all your wonderful deeds.

Psalm 26:2 Test me, LORD, and try me, examine my heart and my mind;

Psalm 34:18 The LORD is close to the broken-hearted and saves those who are crushed in spirit.

Matthew 5:8 Blessed are the pure in heart, for they will see God.

Mark 6:52 for they had not understood about the loaves; their hearts were hardened.

Psalm 24:4 The one who has clean hands and a pure heart, who does not trust in an idol or swear by a false god.

Psalm 19:14 May these words of my mouth and this meditation of my heart be pleasing in your sight, LORD, my Rock and my Redeemer.

Psalm 119:1Blessed are those whose ways are blameless, who walk according to the law of the LORD.

> If the condition of our hearts were not important to God there wouldn't be this many scriptures dealing with it. I use to think that our hearts were our spirits which at the new birth is perfect in the sight of God and sinless. But the terms broken-hearted hard hearted doubt in heart pure in heart makes me wonder.

Word study mode kicks in so look up in strong concordance meaning of heart in mark 11:23

2588. kardia ▶

Strong's Concordance

kardia: heart

Original Word: καρδία, ας, ἡ
Part of Speech: Noun, Feminine
Transliteration: kardia
Phonetic Spelling: (kar-dee'-ah)
Definition: heart
Usage: lit: the heart; mind, character, inner self, will, intention, center.

HELPS Word-studies

2588 *kardía – heart*; "the *affective* center of our being" and the *capacity of moral preference* (*volitional desire, choice*; see P. Hughs, *2 Cor*, 354); "*desire*-producer that makes us tick" (G. Archer), i.e. our "desire-

decisions" that establish who we really are.

[*Heart* (2588 */kardía*) is mentioned over 800 times in Scripture, but *never* referring to the literal physical pump that drives the blood. That is, "heart" is *only used figuratively* (both in the OT and NT.

Interestingly sheds a whole new light on things. Let's continue our research and study to see if we can get revelation and blessing to invade our lives.

2 OPINIONS

Opinions, this is something everyone has and is quick to express theirs. I heard a preacher once say God is not interested in our opinions. I don't get offended at such comments because when I hear them I automatically think, "of course He don't, He is all knowing all seeing and unlimited and I barely have a clue about my own sphere of influence." That's surface thinking and put's God beyond the scope of having a relationship with me. So I decided to look at it again with relationship between creator and creation in mind.

First thing I asked myself was where do opinions come from? Opinions come through interaction with others within the sphere of our influence. They come through our five senses. Humans have a multitude of **senses.** Sight, hearing, taste, smell, and touch are the **five** traditionally recognized.

Then I clued in God wasn't in the equation and probably eighty to ninety percent of our opinions are formed from the lower kingdom the natural fallen world. In our relationship with the Holy Spirit who is in the earth today leading guiding and brings revelation, He desires a change to happen in us. I want to share an event that happened to me as a young Christian to help me understand speaking from the lower kingdom.

I would get up very early in the morning before anyone else. The living room was a quiet deserted and comfortable place to pray. I would start my prayers with, "good morning Father God how's heaven." Then I would pray for pastor's government leader's family and neighbors. I had a routine of this day after day. Then one morning after I asked the heavenly Father how's heaven? He quickly responded "heaven's great how is earth? "I was stunned and didn't pray that day. Instead I asked older Christians why God would ask me that. I got a lot of religious sounding opinions that never settled in my thinking. So being super intelligent and wise (hahaha) I did what I should have done firstly. I asked God why did you ask me how is earth? He responded, "I was talking to you the same way you were talking to me. You asked me how is heaven so I asked you how is earth." Then suddenly an epiphany or revelation hit my mind 2 Peter 1: [19] We also have the prophetic message as something completely reliable, and you will do well to pay attention to it, as to a light shining in a dark place, until the day dawns and the morning star rises in your hearts

I understood God comes to us on our level with the intent of ringing us up to his level.

We can be at another level when it comes to expressing our opinions. How you may ask? James 1:19 Know this, my beloved brothers: let every person be quick to hear, slow to speak, slow to anger; So hear what people say and be quick to turn inwards seeking counsel and wisdom from the Holy Spirit before expressing your opinion.

Hebrews 5:12-14 [12]In fact, though by this time you ought to be teachers, you need someone to teach you the elementary truths of God's word all over again. You need milk, not solid food! [13]Anyone, who lives on milk, being still an infant, is not acquainted with the teaching about righteousness. [14]But solid food is for the mature, who by constant use have trained themselves to distinguish good from evil.

3 CHARACTER

There are many meanings of character but I want to use this one for our study.

Character
[ˈkerəktər]
NOUN

1. The mental and moral qualities distinctive to an individual.

   "running away was not in keeping with her character"

   synonyms:

   <u>personality</u> · <u>nature</u> · <u>disposition</u> · <u>temperament</u> · <u>temper</u> · <u>mentality</u> · <u>turn of mind</u> · <u>psychology</u> · <u>psyche</u> · <u>constitution</u> · <u>makeup</u> · <u>make</u> · <u>stamp</u> · <u>mold</u> · <u>cast</u> · <u>persona</u> · <u>attributes</u> · <u>features</u> · <u>qualities</u> · <u>properties</u> · <u>traits</u> · essential quality · essence · sum and substance · <u>individuality</u> · <u>identity</u> · <u>distinctiveness</u> · <u>uniqueness</u> · <u>spirit</u> · <u>ethos</u> · <u>complexion</u> · <u>key</u> · <u>tone</u> · <u>tenor</u> · <u>ambience</u> · <u>air</u> · <u>aura</u> · <u>feel</u> · <u>feeling</u> · <u>vibrations</u> · <u>kidney</u> · <u>humor</u> · <u>grain</u>

We have been given a new nature at the born again experience.

2 Corinthians 5: **17**Therefore, if anyone is in Christ, he is a new creation. The old has passed away; behold, the new has come. **18**All this is from God, who through Christ reconciled us to himself and gave us the ministry of reconciliation; **19**that is, in Christ God was reconciling the world to himself, not counting their trespasses against them, and entrusting to us the message of reconciliation. **20**Therefore, we are ambassadors for Christ, God making his appeal through us. We implore you on behalf of Christ, be reconciled to God. **21**For our sake he made him to be sin who knew no sin, so that in him we might become the righteousness of God.

We are a new creation so the old sin nature should not dominate our thinking or actions, but yet the old nature seems to rear its ugly head now and again.

Romans 7:15-20 New International Version (NIV)
[15] I do not understand what I do. For what I want to do I do not do, but what I hate I do. [16] And if I

do what I do not want to do, I agree that the law is good. [17] As it is, it is no longer I myself who do it, but it is sin living in me. [18] For I know that good itself does not dwell in me, that is, in my sinful nature.[a] For I have the desire to do what is good, but I cannot carry it out. [19] For I do not do the good I want to do, but the evil I do not want to do—this I keep on doing. [20] Now if I do what I do not want to do, it is no longer I who do it, but it is sin living in me that does it.

Problem, problem, problem because the bible says we are like Christ.

1 John 4:17 King James Bible
Herein is our love made perfect, that we may have boldness in the day of judgment: because as he is, so are we in this world.

When I look at myself and judge myself I don't act or look like Christ. How can I change to be more like Jesus Christ?

4 THE MIND

The mind or our thinking centre has to change drastically.

Romans 12 New International Version (NIV)

A Living Sacrifice

12 Therefore, I urge you, brothers and sisters, in view of God's mercy, to offer your bodies as a living sacrifice, holy and pleasing to God—this is your true and proper worship. [2] Do not conform to the pattern of this world, but be transformed by the renewing of your mind. Then you will be able to test and approve what God's will is—his good, pleasing and perfect will.

Our thinking patterns so determine our actions.

Romans 8:6 Contemporary English Version
If our minds are ruled by our desires, we will die. But if our minds are ruled by the Spirit, we will have life and peace.

I lived with a Christian couple for a while and noticed different behavior from what I thought should be norm. Every night after supper the television would come on and would put on a movie that included blasphemy sexual situations and an abundance of violence. I would retire to my room and watch preaching on you tube. One evening I tried putting on a godly show and the man hollered turn that garbage off. I was glad when I was able to move from that place.

What is Jesus to us? We get born again our fire insurance so as to not be thrown into the lake of fire at judgment day, then forget about a relationship with the Holy Spirit? Live our lives according to our natural lustful desires and when we begin to reap the rewards that come with the lifestyle of being carnally minded we run to God for help. In God's mercy he helps us so we thank him and act all religious, maybe take in an extra service we normally don't attend. Then after a period of time we forget and go back to the carnal thinking that got us to the place we didn't want to be.

Romans 8:6-7 King James Version (KJV)

[6] For to be carnally minded is death; but to be spiritually minded is life and peace.

[7] Because the carnal mind is enmity against God: for it is not subject to the law of God, neither indeed can be.

So my question to you is how important do you **think you're thinking patterns are in your relationship with God and people?** What are you going to do to be spiritually minded rather than carnal minded?

5 MY WILL_MOTIVES

My will! The most important will in life. I want things done my way. I want everything my way. I want all people within the sphere of my influence to bow down to my will. Everything in life is about me. Prosperity, health, honor and especially fame and accolades all about me. This is basically the carnal nature at its finest. As Christians we are not exempt from this.

Here is a thought about the definition of time; TIME IS WHEN TWO OPPOSING WILLS ARE IN MOTION AT THE SAME INSTANCE.

Jeremiah 17:9 [9]**The** heart is deceitful above all things and beyond cure. Who can understand it?

My will and my motives come from my heart. I can do acts of charity and kindness and look good in the eyes of men who don't know why I did them. I know of a situation where a person needed a place to live and another person offered him a bedroom to live for the price of a book. When asked why so cheap the man responded so my dad can't stay here on the weekends like he wants to. After a couple of months the demand for money came and it became higher and higher. It became apparent the man didn't want to work and was looking for someone else to pay his mortgage while he sat around visiting with friends. He couldn't find a boss that would submit to his will which dictated the days and hours and type of work he wanted because after all he was a child of God and he had authority over the dark kingdom. You can imagine the jobs he went through. Sad thing this was done in front of church members and bible study groups to show how good and charitable he was. Renting the room out for the price of the book was what was told everyone in the beginning so as to look good in people's eyes. The rest of his actions were done privately and secretly. Our hearts can be so deceptive that our motives though looking good on the outward can be really self-serving and manipulating.

Many times we judge others by their actions while judging ourselves by our intentions.

How can we be free from such attitudes of self-serving and judgments? When my will and motives rule then truth is lost and self-deception reigns rampant.

I wonder what the Lord's Prayer has to say about my will Luke 11 King James Version (KJV) **11** And it came to pass, that, as he was praying in a certain place, when he ceased, one of his disciples said unto him, Lord, teach us to pray, as John also taught his disciples.

² And he said unto them, when ye pray, say, Our Father which art in heaven, Hallowed be thy name. Thy kingdom come. Thy will be done, as in heaven, so in earth.

³ Give us day by day our daily bread.

⁴ And forgive us our sins; for we also forgive every one that is indebted to us. And lead us not into temptation; but deliver us from evil.

The Father's will be done not my will. What about Jesus in the garden?

Matthew 26:36-41 Then Jesus went with his

disciples to a place called Gethsemane, and he said to them, "Sit here while I go over there and pray." 37 He took Peter and the two sons of Zebedee along with him, and he began to be sorrowful and troubled. 38 Then he said to them, "My soul is overwhelmed with sorrow to the point of death. Stay here and keep watch with me." 39 Going a little farther, he fell with his face to the ground and prayed, "My Father, if it is possible, may this cup be taken from me. Yet not **as I will**, but as **you will**." 40 Then he returned to his disciples and found them sleeping. "Could you men not keep watch with me for one hour?" he asked Peter. 41 "Watch and pray so that you will not fall into temptation. The spirit is willing, but the body is weak."

Life isn't about my will but the father's will. How do we make that happen?

The answer starts with this verse.   James 4:7
New King James Version
Therefore submit to God. Resist the devil and he will flee from you.

When we submit to the Holy Spirit we give Him permission in us to change us into the image of Jesus.

1Corinthians 4:5 [5]Therefore judge nothing before the appointed time; wait until the LORD comes. He will bring to light what is hidden in darkness and will expose the motives of the heart. At that time each will receive their praise from God.

Sometimes people come into our lives and show us what not to be like. Other times people give us inspiration to grow in our relationship with the Holy Spirit.

6 OPENING THE BOOK OF YOUR HEART

Opening my heart seems scary for some people. Open up your heart in marriage only to be betrayed and used. Never measuring up to people; always falling short. Can I be sure God won't reject me like some people do? When we become children of God everything changes. We become children of a God who doesn't have love but is love. The entire passage found in 1 John 4:7-21 speaks of God's loving nature. Love is not merely an attribute of God, it is his very nature. God is not only loving, he is fundamentally love. God alone loves in the completeness and perfection of love.

Thus, if God is love and we, his followers, are born of God, then we will also love. God loves us, so we must love one another. A true Christian, one saved by love and filled with God's love, must live in love toward God and others.

In this section of Scripture, we learn that brotherly love is our response to God's love. The Lord teaches believers how to show his love to others, to our friends, family, and even our enemies. God's love is unconditional; his love is very different from the human love we experience with one another because it is not based on feelings. He doesn't love us because we please him. He loves us simply because he is love.

Love is the true test of Christianity. The character of God is rooted in love. We receive God's love in our relationship with him. We experience God's love in our relationships with others.

God's love is a gift. God's love is a life-giving, energizing force. This love was demonstrated in Jesus Christ: "As the Father has loved me, so have I loved you.

Abide in my love" (John 15:9, ESV). When we receive God's love, we are enabled through that love to love others. Satan tries to instill fear in us to prevent us from opening our hearts to God.

2 timothy 1:7 King **James Bible**
For God hath not given us the spirit of fear; but of power, and of love, and of a sound mind.

Christian Standard Bible
For God has not given us a spirit of fear, but one of power, love, and sound judgment.

Contemporary English Version
God's Spirit doesn't make cowards out of us. The Spirit gives us power, love, and self-control.

Satan continually puts thoughts in our head of failure rejection and failure. These thoughts are on replay and will continue over and over again until you do something about them.

2 Corinthians 10:5-7 King James Version (KJV)

[5] Casting down imaginations, and every high thing that exalteth itself against the knowledge of God, and bringing into captivity every thought to the obedience of Christ;

I asked a brother in Christ how his relationship with the Holy Spirit was going and he responded, "As I yield and submit my heart more, more and more the relationship is improving."

Romans 12:2 ESV

Do not be conformed to this world, but be transformed by the renewal of your mind, that by testing you may discern what is the will of God, what is good and acceptable and perfect.

Ephesians 1:18

Ephesians 1:18 Having the eyes of your hearts enlightened, that you may know what is the hope to which he has called you, what are the riches of his glorious inheritance in the saints,

1.   That should be our daily prayer. Pray in the Spirit. "But you, beloved, building yourselves up in your most holy faith and praying in the Holy Spirit...**Jude 1:20**

2.   Fully trust the Lord. "... keep yourselves in the love of God, waiting for the mercy of our Lord Jesus ... **Jude 1:21**

3.   Cultivate Christ's heart. "And have mercy on those who doubt; save others by snatching them out ... Jude 1:22-23

4.   Have the fear of God. "... to others show mercy with fear..." (Jude 23) In our drive to rescue others ...

We are in a war and Satan knows that if we open the book of our heart to God we become an unconquerable enemy blessed by God.

THE MESSAGE BIBLE PSALM 18:24

God rewrote the text of my life when I opened the book of my heart to his eyes.

25 The good people taste your goodness; the whole people taste your health,

26 The true people taste your truth; the bad ones can't figure you out.

27 You take the side of the down-and-out, but the stuck-up you take down a peg.

28 Suddenly, God, you floodlight my life; I'm blazing with glory, God's glory!

7 WORDS AND DESTINY

People don't realize how important words spoken are.

Luke 6:45 English Standard Version
The good person out of the good treasure of his heart produces good, and the evil person out of his evil treasure produces evil, for out of the abundance of the heart his mouth speaks.

What people fail to realize is that you will eventually walk and live what you talk. If your heart is good you will speak life and blessing to all within the sphere of your influence.

WORDS

Words! It is totally amazing that this subject is probably one of the most taught subjects, yet the Body of Christ is still grossly ignorant of the effect words have in our lives. It is time to wake up and realize what is happening here. In the following dream we are going to see the importance and power of words and why Satan would like to control your tongue. This dream started with my wife Carrie and me walking up the sidewalk on our way to church. Upon entering the lobby of the church we noticed the Pastor standing a few feet inside the sanctuary. We thought this was rather strange as the pastor was usually in the lobby greeting people. The pastor was bidding people to come into the sanctuary and take a seat. The look on the pastor's face was very different than the joyful expression he usually carted around. You could see fear in his eyes and a slight trembling of his body. I was wondering why the other people who were filing into the sanctuary were totally oblivious to the pastor's nervous apprehension.

Soon the entire congregation was seated. The pastor made his way to the pulpit and began to speak. About a minute into the pastor's message a sound echoed throughout the sanctuary. The sound was the sound of rifle bolts being snapped into place arming the weapons. I turned around to see the source of the sound. In the balcony of our church were people holding guns of all kinds. They were carrying rifles, shotguns, machine guns, and a variety of other high-powered weapons. This group of people was holding the entire church captive. There were only a few gunmen but the entire congregation sat in fear of these men. These men told the congregation to sit quietly or else they would be shot. I looked around the church and everyone was paralyzed with fear.

Suddenly I began to quote scriptures from the bible. I quoted Isaiah 54:17, "No weapon formed against you shall prosper, and every tongue which raises against you in judgment you shall condemn. This is the heritage of the servants of the Lord, and their righteousness is from me, says the Lord." I also quoted Luke 10:19, "Behold, I give you the authority to trample on serpents and scorpions, and over all the power of the enemy, and nothing shall by any means hurt you."

I quoted these scriptures three or four times, and then I stood to my feet. Turning to face our captors, I continued quoting scriptures. The gunmen started shouting and hollering for me to sit down and shut up or else I would be shot. I use the term gunmen here in a most generic term not implying just males but including females in the term as well. I started to make my way to the balcony still quoting scriptures. I yelled the scriptures so loud, in response to their threats that I blocked out the sounds they were making.

These scriptures exploded in my heart becoming so powerful and overwhelmed me to the degree that the truths they portrayed became the only thing I could comprehend or understand.

The gunmen opened fire upon me with every weapon they had. I kept quoting Isaiah 54:17 and Luke 10:19 as the bullets bounced off my chest. The men were really surprised to see that their weapons had no effect on me. I proceeded to the balcony, disarmed them, and brought them down to the front of the church.

The pastor started preaching with enthusiasm and fire from the core of his being as the gunmen were coming down the aisle toward the front of the church. When the gunmen got to the front of the church the pastor became unglued, preaching with everything he had in him. The Anointing of God was released and after a few minutes some of the gunmen broke down and repented for their actions against the church. When we enquired of the remaining gunmen as to whether or not they would like to repent demonic spirits began to manifest through them. We commanded the devils to leave in the name of Jesus Christ. After the devils left the remaining gunmen repented. This was the end of the dream.

The interpretation of the dream is this; the gunmen are Christians, the rifles and high-powered weapons are the Christian's tongues; the bullets are **WORDS.** The Christians in the balcony represent their position of spirituality they thought they had attained. They believed they were greater in their walk with God than anyone else. They exalted themselves above measure simply because they had an office or a position or title in the church. Their words brought fear and bondage upon all who heard them speak in the church. This was easily accomplished by having the congregation believe their exalted position.

When I stood up and challenged them they felt threatened, unleashing words meant for my destruction. The scriptures I quoted not only protected me but also disarmed them. These people were using their tongues to control the church. By creating an atmosphere of fear and bondage the church remained paralyzed. The Holy Spirit wasn't able to move the way He wanted to in this church because when He would move He be spoken against, especially if it wasn't the way the gunmen thought it should be. The Holy Spirit is a gentleman and will not include us in His moves if we don't want to be involved. He will pass over us and let us have our fear and bondage if we want it. After being brought down from their lofty perch, they were escorted to the front of the church. The pastor preached God's word with authority and power because he himself was set free when these people were removed from their lofty perch. After hearing the Word of God many repented while others had to have the devil cast off of them. Once the devil was gone then all could repent and be set free from their patterns of destruction they were causing.

I believe and have seen this sort of activity happening in many churches today. Some of the people who use their tongues for destruction are simply ignorant of the harm they are doing. When they are quiet long enough to hear God's voice manifested through His Word they will repent. You may have to challenge them to change. We also have those who are so caught up with religion and tradition that blindness has come upon them in part. This type of people looks to the past. When God moved a certain way back then and they had an experience with Him they seem to think that that is the only way God moves and speak against any new thing He may be attempting to do in their church. They like their comfort zones and continually thwart the plan of God by using demeaning destructive words to stop the move of God in their church.

When I realized words play an important part in my life I began to seek the Lord and ask for revelation in this area. Out of the abundance of my heart my tongue will utter and eventually my feet will walk what I talk. Your actions will soon show the world and God what's in your heart. Paul said in **1 Corinthians 11:1** Be imitators of me, even as I also am of Christ. **Philippians 3:17**Join one another in following my example, brothers, and carefully observe those who walk according to the pattern we set for you.

I realized there is a pattern we could follow to be an example of Christ in us and words can create that pattern.

Mark 11:23 [23]"Truly I tell you, if anyone says to this mountain, 'Go, throw yourself into the sea,' and does not doubt in their heart but believes that what they say will happen, it will be done for them.

The mountain in this case is the

condition of my heart; if I chose to believe the words that come from my mouth I can change the condition of my heart. I read the old testament many times and I noticed when the kings spoke words well or bad it affected his entire kingdom. I also noticed when God was going to talk with people He would speak about His character first then what He said was manifested. Hmmm I thought if we are to imitate Christ then what words should I speak in order to have Christ in me manifested rather than carnal flesh me?

I studied the fruit of the Spirit; **Galatians 5:22-26** [22]But the **fruit of** the Spirit is love, joy, peace, forbearance, kindness, goodness, faithfulness, [23]gentleness and self-control. Against such things there is no law. [24]Those who belong to Christ Jesus have crucified the flesh with its passions and desires. [25]Since we live by the Spirit, let us keep in step with **the Spirit**. [26]Let us not become conceited, provoking and envying each other.

I came to the conclusion the fruit of the spirit is the very nature of God and I wanted that in my life. I decided to apply mark 11:23 about believing what I say to the fruit of the spirit. I don't have these attributes I am love, I am joy, I am peace, I am forbearance, I am kindness, I am goodness, I am faithful, I am gentle, I am self-control. Speaking in this manner changed my thinking and attitudes towards others. When I was a delivery person for pizza shops I wanted a parting statement rather than have a good day which was cliché and everybody said it. So after talking to the Holy Spirit this simple phrase dropped in my heart, "enjoy your day." Then I had the thought do a word study on enjoy. I was pleased at the results, the en in front of joy meant to be empowered to have. So when I said enjoy your day I was empowering people to have joy which is the fruit of the spirit. I said this repeatedly for about a year and a half then I noticed a bank teller said that to me as I finished my business. It took that long but it came full circle proving to me that your words can affect others and yourself. My thinking and attitudes have changed where people have said to me they see Jesus in me. That is my agreement with John the Baptist He must increase and I must decrease.

To many people use words to explain their circumstances and situations in life not realizing they will have more of what they say. They should be using words to change their lives and circumstances. I personally believe words are meant to change broken hearted, hard hearted and deceptive hearts into pure hearts before the Lord. What are you saying about yourself and others within the sphere of your influence?

8 DESIRE

What do you desire? When asked that question and answer quickly it will probably be flesh related. The more we speak life and blessing into our lives and the lives of others, we go from fleshly Christians to spiritual Christians.

Psalm 37:3-5 *Do Not Envy Those who Do Wrong*

...**3**Trust in the LORD and do good; dwell in the land and cultivate faithfulness. **4**Delight yourself in the LORD, and He will give you the desires of your heart. **5**Commit your way to the LORD; trust in Him, and He will do it. **6**He will bring forth your righteousness like the dawn, your justice like the noonday sun. **7**Be still before the LORD and wait patiently for Him; fret not when men prosper in their ways, when they carry out wicked schemes. **8**Refrain from anger and abandon wrath; do not fret—it can only bring harm.

Philippians 3:9-10 *Knowing Christ Above All Else*

...**9**and be found in Him, not having my own righteousness from the law, but that which is through faith in Christ, the righteousness from God on the basis of faith. **10**I want to know Christ and the power of His resurrection and the fellowship of His sufferings, being conformed to Him in His death, **11**and so, somehow, to attain to the resurrection from the dead.

Romans 8:17

And if we are children, then we are heirs: heirs of God and co-heirs with Christ--if indeed we suffer with Him, so that we may also be glorified with Him

The more we fellowship with the Holy Spirit the more intimacy begins to develop. Soon an overwhelming love and fear will develop you. Fear not in being scared but an overwhelming respect and adoration that you don't want to say or do anything that will hurt him. As you continue your daily fellowship; not long winded elegant prayers that are religious sounding at best and filled with unbelief, but chatting about day's events. Talking about your job, shopping and even the weather you will grow in your relationship and have a greater understanding of how he thinks.

I will share two conversations I had with the Holy Spirit about the weather. The first time we had many days of rain and too much just wasn't a blessing. It finally stopped for a couple of hours but the forecast was for more rain coming in. I sat on my balcony and watched a thunder head moving in from the west so I asked God if He would get rid of it for us. I was surprised when I heard in my spirit "you do it." We were learning About authority in church so I thought I would give it a shot. I spoke to the thunder head and said I command you in the name of Jesus to go back west and drop your load over the ocean. I totally expected it to happen and wasn't surprised when the wind changed direction and the cloud moved west. I thanked God went inside and enjoyed nice sunny weather for a few weeks. The second time my cousin and I were doing a roofing Job and it became windy creating a difficult time to work. I prayed and asked God if He would stop the wind so we could finish the job. Instantly the wind stopped and became so calm you could blow smoke rings in the air and watch them for ten minutes. We finished the job and praised God for his help. The next day another job and the wind came up again so I asked God to stop it expecting the same thing. Pleasantly surprised I heard not today I am seeding the earth. I looked around and I could see pollen carrying seeds of plants flowers and other vegetation flying through the air. I mentioned it to my cousin and we praised God for a revelation of Him at work in the earth and nature. We finished the job just a bit later because of the wind.

Fellowship with the Holy Spirit will cause you to become more Christ like in nature for that is his assignment in the earth. I believe part of the Holy Spirit's work is to help you bring **Matthew 5:8** "Blessed are the pure in heart, for they shall see God, to fulfillment in your life. Not only see God the Father one day but see God at work in people's lives. Recognize their anointing's and gifts in their lives, honoring them and encouraging them to fulfill their destinies in

Christ.

My desire is to be more like Christ; hating sin but loving the sinner. To build strengthen and encourage His body to grow in relationship with Him and fulfill their destinies in Christ. If God showed us our destinies we would be flabbergasted because it's more than we can imagine or hope for.

Ephesians 2:7 in order that he may show in coming ages the super abounding riches of his grace in kindness toward us in Christ Jesus.

We are in the church age now. In eternity future how many and what kind of ages does God the Father have planned? Your heart condition matters, so go to the Holy Spirit and together work on creating a pure heart in you.

PROLOGUE

Everybody is interested in the future. Questions are asked and internalized, meditated on and depending on the outcome of the meditation, reaction results. Our reactions are either fear based or faith based depending on the subject meditated on. I Have always been interested in the love and personality of God the Father. I hope you enjoy my exploration into this subject

ABOUT THE AUTHOR

BIO

William carries the anointing of a prophet and psalmist. He is also a Bible teacher, author and international speaker. He operates in all of the Spiritual gifts. He uses the gifts as the Holy Spirit wills. One of William's great desires is to lead others to Christ and to follow Holy Spirit wherever He leads.

YOU CAN VISIT MY WEBSITE
WWW.PSALMISTWILLIAM.CA
FOR ENCOURAGING PSALMS AND TO BUY OTHER BOOKS I HAVE WRITTEN